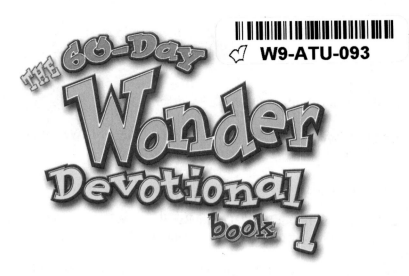

The 66-Day Wonder Devotional book 1

What a God!

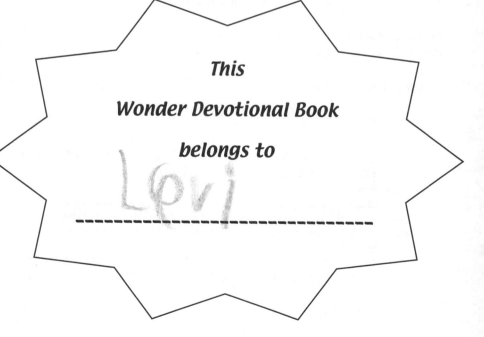

This

Wonder Devotional Book

belongs to

Levi

Child Evangelism Fellowship Inc.

Project Coordinator: Lynda E. Pongracz

General Editors: Lynda E. Pongracz, Dr. Martha J. Wright and Brenda J. Hanson

Text Editor: Cynthia H. Channell

Development Team: Lisa J. Deam, Rev. Jerry W. Hanson, Deborah Koenig, Lynda E. Pongracz, Terrie Taylor, Elaine Weller

Writers: Dr. Martha J. Wright, Sharron R. Oyer and Jennifer Haaijer

Theological Consultants: Rev. Arthur Cobb, M. Joe Cox, Rev. Dair Hileman, Dr. Timothy D. Martin, Rev. Jim Neigh, Rev. John Romano, Rev. D. Bruce Seymour, Rev. Brian Thom and Dr. Mark Yelderman

Editorial Committee: Patricia R. Johann, Cheryl L. Oetting, Lynda E. Pongracz and Dr. Martha J. Wright

Graphic Design: Marvin R. White III and Thomas S. Bates

Cover: Stephen R. Bates

Special thanks to *Child Evangelism Fellowship*® President Reese Kauffman, Marshall J. Pennell, Stephen Bates, Dr. A. A. Baker and the *CEF*® worldwide family for their input, prayers and support.

The 60-Day Wonder Devotional Book 1: What a God!

ISBN 1-55976-118-0

Printed in the United States of America

Are you ready for an adventure?

Getting to know God is a great adventure! Did you know that God wants you to spend time with Him each day? He does! We call that a "quiet time." It's when you read and think about God and talk to Him.

This devotional book will help you in your quiet time for the next two months. Choose a special time each day—maybe when you first wake up in the morning or just before you go to bed at night. Be sure you have this book, a pen or pencil and your Bible if you have one.

Here's what to do each day!

 Talk to God. Ask Him to help you understand what you read.

 Read the Bible memory verse. It's at the top of the page. If you have a Bible, look up the verse. See how quickly you can memorize God's message for you!

 Read the devotional. Each one will answer an important question. Take your time reading and think about what it says.

 Write your answer. Read the question following the devotional and write your answer. Writing helps you remember!

 Talk to God again. Use the prayer starter at the end of each devotional to help you. Thank God for all He does for you. Talk to Him about problems and ask Him to help you or someone you love. God looks forward to hearing from you!

 Activity Pages! There are two fun activity pages to figure out. See how much you can remember from what you've read!

Wow! Are you ready to get to know God? Don't wait another day. Turn to devotional #1 and get started on your adventure!

Who Is God?

The heavens declare the glory of God; the skies proclaim the work of his hands. Psalm 19:1

Have you ever wondered who God is? Some people think that God is an old man who lives in the clouds. Others think that He is someone who causes bad things to happen when we do something wrong. Some people think that the sun and stars are gods because they give us light. Other people say, "There is no God."

The Bible, God's Word, tells us that the one true God is a Spirit. He doesn't have a body like you and me. That's why we can't see Him, but He sees and hears and loves. God is everywhere. God is the Creator. He made the world and everything in it—the mountains, oceans and animals. God also made you and me. We are His most special creation, and He loves us very much.

Grown-ups and children all need God. All people have something inside telling them there is a God. This book will help you learn about God. You will learn how great and wonderful God is. You will learn how to love Him and live closer to Him even though you cannot see Him. Are you ready for the exciting adventure of getting to know God?

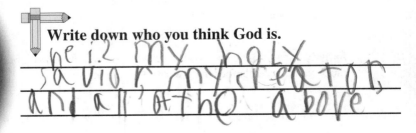

Write down who you think God is.

he is my holy savior, my creator, and all of the above

You can pray:

Dear God, thank You for being a great God! Thank You for creating me. Help me to learn more about You so that I will love You. In Jesus' name. Amen.

2 Are There Many Gods?

The heavens declare the glory of God; the skies proclaim the work of his hands. **Psalm 19:1**

Some people worship many gods, but the Bible tells us that there is only one true living God. The Bible says that God is three Persons, but He is one God. That is something we cannot understand. The Bible teaches us about God the Father, God the Son and God the Holy Spirit. They are the three Persons.

God the Father lives in Heaven, but He is everywhere. He is holy and without sin. God rules over His creation. He is in control of all things. He loves everyone.

Jesus is God the Son. He died for our sins and rose again. All people can have their sins forgiven if they trust in Him as their personal Savior. After Jesus rose from the dead, He went up into Heaven. Now Jesus is with His Father, God.

God the Holy Spirit came to Earth after Jesus returned to Heaven. He helps people to know that they are sinners. He then comes to live in the hearts of those who trust in Jesus. The Holy Spirit also helps us understand God's Word, the Bible.

God the Father, God the Son and God the Holy Spirit—they are the Trinity. They are three in one. All agree completely.

Can you name the three Persons of the Trinity?

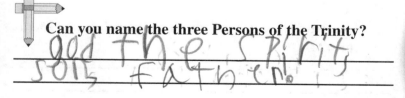

god the spirit son father

You can pray:

Dear God, thank You for sending Jesus to be our Savior. Thank You for the Holy Spirit who lives in the hearts of those who believe in Jesus. In Jesus' name. Amen.

How Old Is God?

The heavens declare the glory of God; the skies proclaim the work of his hands. **Psalm 19:1**

Maybe you think that because God created the world, He must be at least two million years old! Wrong! God is eternal. There never has been a time that He has not existed. There will never be a time when He will stop existing.

Think of a circle. You cannot tell where the circle begins and ends. It is one continuous ring. A circle can remind you that God is eternal. The Father, the Son and the Holy Spirit always have existed and always will. We have a hard time imagining that.

The Bible says "…from everlasting to everlasting you are God" (Psalm 90:2). How long is that? It is forever. If you have believed in Jesus as your Savior, God has given you eternal life. Will it ever end? No! You are God's child forever! God wants to guide your life. Because He is eternal—He always has been and always will be—He can see what has happened, what is happening and what will happen. What a guide to have! How great God is!

Will you trust your Heavenly Father who is eternal? You cannot see what will happen in the future, but God sees and wants to direct your life.

How would you explain to a friend that God is eternal?

he Lives forever and ever!

You can pray:

Dear God, thank You that You will never leave me because You are eternal. Thank You that I can trust You because You will always be there for me. In Jesus' name. Amen.

# **H**ow Powerful Is God?

 The heavens declare the glory of God; the skies proclaim the work of his hands. **Psalm 19:1**

The 4 1/2 million-pound spaceship Columbia blasted off with a long fiery tail. Two minutes later, it had reached an altitude of 23 miles. It circled the globe at 17,000 miles per hour. Imagine the power that it took to push that huge rocket through space at that speed!

Did you know God is more powerful than that? The Bible says, "The Lord is…great in power…" (Nahum 1:3). He made the heavens and Earth. God spoke and it was there! He is almighty. He rules over all nations. God's power has no limits. He can make anything happen.

The Bible tells about Abraham and Sarah. God promised them that they would have many children, but no children were born. One day, God sent an angel to Abraham when he and Sarah were almost 100 years old. The angel told him that the following year Sarah would have a son. That was impossible! When Sarah laughed, the angel said, "Is anything too hard for the Lord?" (Genesis 18:14). Sure enough, Sarah had a son! Because God is all-powerful, He could make this impossible thing happen. The next time you have a problem, remember that God is very powerful and wants to help you.

 Can you name some ways that God is powerful?

_____

_____

_____

You can pray:

 Dear God, You are the mighty God! Help me to trust You when I have a problem that seems impossible. Help me to remember that You are Ruler over all. In Jesus' name.

Why Did God Create People?

...Just as sin entered the world through one man, and death through sin, and in this way death came to all men, because all sinned. **Romans 5:12**

Have you ever wondered where all the people on Earth came from? God made them all! After God made the beautiful Earth, He made one man. He made that man out of the dust of the Earth and breathed life into him. God called that man Adam. Later, God caused Adam to sleep and took a rib from his side to make the first woman. God gave Adam this woman, Eve, to be his wife. Adam and Eve lived in the beautiful garden that God made.

Soon Adam and Eve had many children. When the children grew up, they had children. Soon there were many people on the Earth. Today there are so many people it is hard to count them all!

God did not create people because He was lonely. He made us so that we could love Him and praise Him. The Bible says, "Great is the Lord, and most worthy of praise…" (Psalm 48:1). God wants people to praise Him because He is great and good.

When you see all that God has made, you can say, "How great God is!" You can praise Him when you pray. Tell Him that you love Him and that you need Him. You can never praise God enough.

 Write down three things you can praise God for today.

_____

_____

You can pray:

Dear God, thank You for creating me. I love You and praise You because You are so great. In Jesus' name. Amen.

 **H** ow Did Sin Enter the World?

...Just as sin entered the world through one man, and death through sin, and in this way death came to all men, because all sinned. **Romans 5:12**

God made everything in the world beautiful and good. But many things in our world are not beautiful and good anymore. There is sickness, sadness, fighting and killing. Why did things go so wrong?

God placed the very first people, Adam and Eve, in the garden. He told them they were not to eat the fruit from one certain tree or they would die. God's enemy, Satan, tricked Eve into eating the fruit. Adam ate it, too. In choosing to disobey God, they sinned.

God told Adam that they would have to leave the garden. They would have pain and sickness and their bodies would die. Sin separated Adam and Eve from God, who is holy and perfect.

Ever since Adam and Eve sinned, everyone is born sinful and separated from God. The Bible says, "For all have sinned…" (Romans 3:23). Sin is thinking, saying or doing things that break God's laws. It is sin in your heart that causes you to do bad things. You cannot get rid of your sin by yourself. You deserve to be punished for your sin. Only God can forgive you so that you will not be separated from Him forever.

What sad things happened when Adam and Eve sinned?

_____

_____

_____

You can pray:

Dear God, thank You that You love me even though I have sinned. Thank You that You forgive me. In Jesus' name. Amen.

# What Did God Do about Sin?

...Just as sin entered the world through one man, and death through sin, and in this way death came to all men, because all sinned. **Romans 5:12**

The most wonderful story in all the world is the story of what God did so that we could have our sins forgiven.

After Adam and Eve sinned, God promised to send a Savior. You and I know today that the Savior is the Lord Jesus Christ, God's only Son. He was born into this world as a baby. When He became a man, He gave Himself to die on the cross for our sins.

As Jesus died, God placed upon Him the sins of the whole world. The Bible says, "God made him who had no sin to be sin for us…" (2 Corinthians 5:21). Jesus did not deserve to die. He had no sin of His own. He was perfect, but He took your place on the cross. If Jesus had not given His precious blood to take your punishment, you could never be forgiven of your sins. Jesus died and was buried. Three days later God brought Him back to life. Jesus later returned to Heaven where He is alive today. God kept His promise to pay for sin. He sent His own beloved Son to be the Savior of the world.

Write down why you think Jesus had to die.

_____

_____

_____

You can pray:

Dear God, thank You for sending Your only Son, Jesus, to die on the cross for me. Thank You for Your great love. In Jesus' name. Amen.

How Can I Be Forgiven?

...Just as sin entered the world through one man, and death through sin, and in this way death came to all men, because all sinned. **Romans 5:12**

Now you know Jesus died for your sins. Are you wondering how you can be forgiven? The Bible says that Jesus is the only way to God. "I [Jesus] am the way and the truth and the life. No one comes to the Father [God] except through me" (John 14:6).

Jesus wants to be your Savior. You cannot save yourself from sin. You're not saved from sin's punishment by doing good things. You can't be forgiven by saying prayers, giving money or trying to please God. God says there is only one way, and that is through His Son, Jesus.

The Bible says, " ...Believe in the Lord Jesus, and you will be saved..." (Acts 16:31). To believe means to trust completely in the Lord Jesus. His death on the cross is the only payment for your sins that God will accept. When you choose to trust in the Lord Jesus as your Savior, God says you are forgiven. You are rescued from the punishment of your sins. You will not be separated from God in a place of punishment when you die. You'll live with God forever in Heaven someday.

What do you need to believe to be forgiven of your sins?

_____

_____

_____

You can pray:

Dear God, I know that I'm a sinner. I believe in Your Son, Jesus, who died to take the punishment for my sins and rose again. I want Jesus to be my Savior. In Jesus' name. Amen.

I s God Really Perfect?

 ...just as he who called you is holy, so be holy in all you do. **1 Peter 1:15**

Do you know someone who never does anything wrong or never makes a mistake? Certain people have searched for many years for someone who is perfect. They never found such a person.

The Bible says in 1 John 1:5, "...God is light; in him there is no darkness at all." This verse means that God is holy and pure. There is no sin at all in Him. There is not even one little bit of badness in God. He is set apart from sin—set apart from all that is evil or bad. God and sin are opposites like light and darkness. God is holy. The Father is holy; the Son, the Lord Jesus Christ, is holy; the Holy Spirit is holy.

There is someone who is perfect— that is God! Only God is perfect. We have all sinned and sin separates us from God. Because God is holy, He has to punish sin. But He gave His Son to die for sin so that we could be forgiven and made holy. When you believed in Jesus as your Savior, you were forgiven of your sins and made holy before God. Aren't you glad?

 How are we different from God?

_____

_____

_____

You can pray:

 Dear God, You are holy and perfect. You alone are good. Thank You that I can come to You as a holy God through the Lord Jesus, who is my Savior. In Jesus' name. Amen.

16 What Does It Mean That God Is Holy?

...just as he who called you is holy, so be holy in all you do.
1 Peter 1:15

Isaiah was one of God's great prophets. God also spoke to Isaiah. God told Isaiah to tell people that one day the Savior of the world would come.

One day God spoke to Isaiah in a vision. A vision is like a dream. Isaiah said that he saw God seated on a throne, high and exalted. Above God were angels. The angels called out to each other, "Holy, holy, holy is the Lord Almighty; the whole earth is full of his glory" (Isaiah 6:3). When Isaiah saw the vision, he was afraid. He saw how sinful he was compared to God. The vision helped him to see that God is holy.

What does it mean that God is holy? He is 100% pure. He never sins—He is perfect. God always does what is right. He is completely good. God hates sin.

If we are sinners, how can we pray to God? God wants us to talk to Him. He told Isaiah not to be afraid. He also tells us not to be afraid. When we believe in the Lord Jesus as our Savior, He takes our sin away and makes us clean so that we can talk to God who is holy.

What do you think it means that God is holy?

_____

_____

_____

You can pray:

Dear God, You are a holy God. Thank You that the Lord Jesus has taken away my sin so that I can pray to You. In Jesus' name. Amen.

Does God Expect Me to Be Holy?

 But just as he who called you is holy, so be holy in all you do. **1 Peter 1:15**

When the prophet Isaiah saw the vision of God and the angels covering their faces in reverence, he saw how holy God is. If you were Isaiah, what would you be thinking? Maybe you would think about how sinful you really are.

If you have trusted in Jesus as your Savior, God expects you to live a clean life. He expects you to be holy. You have a choice. You can give in to sin or you can choose God's way. God will help you to say "no" to sin. He expects you to obey His Word, the Bible, and do what is right. God expects you to tell the truth and always be kind, loving and patient with others. He wants you to be honest and to behave in a way that pleases Him.

Remember that God lives in you to give you the power to live a clean, holy life and to not sin. When you do sin, however, think about how holy God is. Confess your sin to Him right away. God says if you will confess your sins—that is tell Him about the wrong you have done—He will forgive you (1 John 1:9). Will you choose to be holy?

 In what ways does God want you to be holy?

_____

_____

_____

You can pray:

 Dear God, thank You that You are a holy God. Please give me the power to live a holy life. In Jesus' name. Amen.

12 Who's in Charge?

But just as he who called you is holy, so be holy in all you do. **1 Peter 1:15**

Has your mother ever said to you, "You're in charge?" When you're put in charge of something, you are like a king reigning over it. You have control and are responsible for seeing that the assignment is carried out.

Have you ever wondered who's in charge of the world? The Bible tells us that God is sovereign. That means He is in charge or in control of all things. He is the highest ruler. No one is over God. God reigns over everything and everybody all the time. Nothing can happen unless God allows it to happen. He is in control of everything day and night—24 hours a day, seven days a week, 52 weeks a year. He never sleeps or goes away on vacation.

How long will God reign? The Bible says, "The Lord will reign for ever and ever" (Exodus 15:18). God was always in control and He always will be in control. What does that mean for you? No matter what happens in your life, you don't have to be afraid or upset because God is in control. He loves you, and He wants you to trust Him completely. God is the greatest. He is sovereign. He is the King of kings.

What does it mean that God is sovereign?

_____

_____

_____

You can pray:

Dear God, I praise You because You are in control of all things. Help me to trust You each day. In Jesus' name. Amen.

What Are God's Rules for Us?

But just as he who called you is holy, so be holy in all you do. **1 Peter 1:15**

Long ago God gave His people ten special laws to show them how holy He is and how sinful people are. The laws also tell us how God wants His people to live. We call these laws the Ten Commandments:

• **You shall have no other gods before me.** (Worship God alone.)
• **You shall not make for yourself an idol.** (Don't let anything take God's place in your life.)
• **You shall not misuse the name of the Lord your God.** (Only use God's name with respect.)
• **Remember the Sabbath day by keeping it holy.** (One day a week is to rest and worship God.)

• **Honor your father and your mother.** (Treat your parents with respect.)
• **You shall not murder.** (Protect life; never take life away.)
• **You shall not commit adultery.** (Married people are to be true to each other.)
• **You shall not steal.** (Don't take something that is not your own.)
• **You shall not give false testimony.** (Don't lie; tell the whole truth.)
• **You shall not covet.** (Don't want things that belong to others.)

When God spoke these commandments the people were afraid. But Moses, their leader, explained that God was showing them how great He is in order to keep them from sinning. The Israelites said they would obey God. Will you?

Why did God give the Ten Commandments?

_____

_____

You can pray:

Dear God, I want to live for You by keeping Your laws. Help me to do what is right every day. In Jesus' name. Amen.

14

Is God Sovereign over Me?

But just as he who called you is holy, so be holy in all you do. **1 Peter 1:15**

God is sovereign—He is always in control. God does whatever pleases Him. He decides whether we can do what we have planned. He has total control over all people. Nothing that happens in our lives is ever out of God's control.

Have you ever thought that things in your life are out of control? Maybe someone you love has been injured in an accident or died of a terrible disease. Perhaps your family is having a hard time because one or both of your parents have lost their jobs. Maybe someone is being mean to you or treating you unfairly. When you are sick, or when troubles come, you must believe that God loves you and that everything is under His control. He will do what is best for you even though you may not think the situation is good.

The Bible says, "And we know that in all things God works for the good of those who love him" (Romans 8:28). Nothing that happens to you is too small for God not to know about. Nothing is too big for Him to control it. When you can't understand why things happen, just remember that God is in control. You can trust your loving Heavenly Father.

What should you remember when you are going through difficult situations?

_____

_____

_____

You can pray:

Dear God, thank You that You are in control of my life. Help me to remember that You love me and will do what is best for me. In Jesus' name. Amen.

Does My Life Show That God Is in Charge?

 But just as he who called you is holy, so be holy in all you do. **1 Peter 1:15**

God never promised that His children would have a life free from problems and pain. God allows difficult things to happen in our lives as He carries out His plan for us.

It is just as important to trust God as it is to obey Him. When you do not trust God, you are doubting that He is in control and that He is good. God wants you to learn to trust Him every day, all day. He wants you to trust Him in the good times and the difficult ones. Trusting God means believing with all your heart that He is in control and that He is doing what is best for you.

How does your life show that God is in charge? When you are facing a problem, your first response should be to trust God (rely on Him). You can trust Him because you know that God has allowed the problem for a certain reason. Talk to God in prayer and tell Him your problems. As you trust God, He will give you peace, a calmness on the inside. Thank Him for working in your life to make you more like Jesus.

 Why is it important for you to trust God?

_____

_____

_____

You can pray:

 Dear God, help me to trust You in the good times and the difficult ones. Thank You for Your peace. In Jesus' name. Amen.

16 Why Does God Punish Sinners?

Give thanks to the LORD, for he is good; his love endures forever. **Psalm 118:1**

Have you ever said, "That's not fair?" No one can ever say that of God. God is always fair (or just) in everything He does. The Bible says that God "does no wrong, upright and just is he" (Deuteronomy 32:4). God is our judge, and He judges fairly.

Since Adam and Eve, everyone is born into this world with a "want to" to sin. God is holy; He hates sin. He cannot let people do wrong without punishing them because He is just and fair. The Bible says, "For the wages of sin is death..." (Romans 6:23). Wages are what we earn for what we do. What do we earn for sin? Yes, death. God said that because of sin we deserve to be separated from Him forever. That's the punishment our just God placed on sin. It is called eternal death.

But God sent His only Son, the Lord Jesus Christ, to die on the cross and take the punishment we deserve for sin. People who reject the Lord Jesus will be lost forever in a terrible place called Hell. All who believe in Jesus as their Savior are saved from the punishment they deserve (Acts 16:31).

How does God punish sinners?

_____

_____

_____

You can pray:

Dear God, You are always fair in everything you do. Thank You that Jesus took the punishment that I deserve for sin so that I can be saved. In Jesus' name. Amen.

How Much Does God Love Me?

Give thanks to the LORD, for he is good; his love endures forever. **Psalm 118:1**

You know what love is, don't you? When you love someone, you want to be near him. You want to take care of him and do nice things for him. You're quick to forgive him if he does something wrong.

God's love is so much greater and more wonderful than the love we have for other people. God says in Jeremiah 31:3, "I have loved you with an everlasting love." God's love is so great that it lasts forever! His love for you will never end.

There was never a time that God didn't love you. He loved you even before you were born. He knew exactly when you would be born, what color hair and eyes you would have and who your parents would be. He loves you so much that He wants the best for you.

God has so much love that He sent His perfect, only Son, the Lord Jesus, to die in your place on the cross. Jesus' death on the cross is the greatest picture of God's love. He has promised that if you believe in Jesus as your Savior, He will someday take you to Heaven to live with Him forever. Can you see how much God loves you?

 In what ways does God show He loves you?

_____

_____

_____

You can pray:

 Dear God, thank You for Your great love for me. Help me to love You and give You my best. In Jesus' name. Amen.

18 What Is God's Grace?

Give thanks to the LORD, for he is good; his love endures forever. **Psalm 118:1**

Have you ever received a gift you didn't deserve? The gift was given to you out of love. God is so great that He gives us His grace because of His love for us.

Grace is God showing His love to you even though you don't deserve it. You can't earn God's grace. You do not deserve to be saved from sin and to have eternal life. But God showed His grace by saving you from sin's punishment when you trusted in Jesus as your Savior. God also shows His grace by giving you strength and guidance, and by taking care of you each day. God, by His grace, gives you strength to handle difficult problems in your life. Isn't God's grace wonderful?

If you know Jesus as your Savior, you can be thankful that God saved you by His grace. The Bible says, "For it is by grace you have been saved, through faith..." (Ephesians 2:8). You can also depend on God each day for the grace you need to live for Him. Because God shows His grace to you, you should show His grace to others. Have you ever thanked God for His grace in your life?

How does God show His grace to you?

_____

_____

_____

You can pray:

Dear God, thank You for saving me by Your grace. Thank You, too, for the blessings I do not deserve that You give me each day. In Jesus' name. Amen.

What Is God's Mercy? 19

Give thanks to the LORD, for he is good; his love endures forever. **Psalm 118:1**

Have you ever thought about how merciful God is? The Bible says, "The Lord is compassionate [merciful] and gracious...he does not treat us as our sins deserve..." (Psalm 103:8-10).

Mercy is willingly forgiving someone who has done wrong rather than punishing him. It is showing kindness, especially when it is not deserved. That's what God has done for you. Instead of giving you the punishment you deserve for your sin, God in His mercy forgave you when you believed in Jesus as your Savior.

God shows mercy— kindness and love—to you every day in many ways, even though you don't deserve it. He provides for your needs. He hears and answers your prayers.

Now God expects you to be merciful to others. You can be kind and help those in need. You shouldn't look down on others or judge them. Being merciful may mean being a friend to someone others reject. It means being patient with younger brothers or sisters, even when they bother you.

God promises a special blessing to those who are kind and merciful. They will receive mercy. So if you show mercy, don't be surprised when others are merciful to you.

 Why should you show mercy to others?

_____

_____

You can pray:

Dear God, thank You for showing me Your mercy and grace that I don't deserve. Help me to be merciful to others. In Jesus' name. Amen.

26 Why Do Good Things Happen to Bad People?

Give thanks to the LORD, for he is good; his love endures forever. **Psalm 118:1**

Why do people who don't love God sometimes have so many good things happen to them? Maybe they have a lot of money or fame. Yet, some people who love God have so many struggles. It just doesn't seem fair.

God is sovereign, remember? He is in control of all things, including the lives of those who reject Him. God directs their lives according to His purpose and plan. Proverbs 16:9 says, "In his heart a man plans his course, but the LORD determines his steps." God allows people to make their own choices, yet they eventually do what God planned that they would do.

Sometimes it seems so unfair when we see good things happen to bad people. God allows these things to happen because of His mercy and grace. But God is just. One day, each person will stand before Him. Those who have not believed in God's Son, the Lord Jesus, will be punished for their unbelief. Those who have trusted in Jesus as their Savior will be rewarded. Many who have not had very much in this world, will be rich in Heaven!

Don't be jealous of others who have more than you do. Thank God for what you have and for what He allows in your life—both good and bad. He loves you and is in control of everything that happens.

Why do good things happen to bad people?

_____

_____

You can pray:

Dear God, thank You for being so good. Help me to trust what You are doing in my life and in the lives of other people. In Jesus' name. Amen.

Will God Ever Let Me Down**?**

Give thanks to the LORD, for he is good; his love endures forever. **Psalm 118:1**

Has someone ever broken a promise to you? You were really counting on someone and he let you down. Maybe you have wondered who you can really depend on.

The Bible says that there is someone who will never let you down, who will never break His promises to you—that is God! God will always be faithful to His Word and to every promise He has made in it. Since God is perfect, He cannot fail you even one time! The Bible says, "Know therefore that the LORD your God is God;

he is the faithful God..." (Deuteronomy 7:9). That truth should give you peace and confidence as you live each day.

What if you are unfaithful to God? What if you let Him down? Will He still be faithful to you? Will He let you down? The amazing thing about God is that even though we are unfaithful to Him, He will be continually faithful to us. When things are not going as you would like and you have problems that seem out of control, you can be confident that God will never let you down. Thank Him for standing with you and being faithful each day.

 How do you know God will never let you down?

_____

_____

_____

You can pray:

Dear God, thank You that You will always be with me and will never let me down. Thank You for being faithful each day. In Jesus' name. Amen.

Can I Really Believe God?

Give thanks to the LORD, for he is good; his love endures forever. **Psalm 118:1**

Has anybody ever lied to you? It is hard to believe people when it seems as if everyone lies from time to time. In many different situations people often ask, "What is the truth?"

God is all truth—He never lies. God sees and knows all things as they really are. The Bible says that "God is not a man, that he should lie…" (Numbers 23:19). Because God is holy (without sin), He could not be anything else but true.

Not only God Himself is truth, but His Word, the Bible, is the truth. His Word is totally trustworthy. Psalm 119:151 says that all the commands of the Lord are true. If you know Jesus as your Savior, you can trust God completely as you obey everything He says in His Word. God's promises are true. He has always kept His promises from the beginning of time. Many years ago God made a promise to a man named Noah never again to destroy the world with a flood (Genesis 9:11-13). When you see a rainbow, you can remember that God is Truth. He kept His promise to Noah, and He will keep His promise to you. You can believe with all your heart in the God of Truth.

Why can you believe what God says?

_____

_____

_____

You can pray:

Dear God, thank You that You are Truth and that I can believe what You say. In Jesus' name. Amen.

Does God Know Everything?

Give thanks to the LORD, for he is good; his love endures forever. **Psalm 118:1**

Have you ever met someone who thinks he knows it all? Maybe he can answer all your questions or get an "A" on tests at school. You think he's the smartest person in the world. But, no matter how much your friend knows, he doesn't know anything compared to God. God knows everything.

God has all knowledge—He knows everything in the whole world. Because God is all-wise, He uses all of that information in the best way possible. Since God made and understands all things, He has perfect plans. He knows what is best for you. In His wisdom, He carries out His plans for you. God knows exactly what He is allowing in your life even though some things may be hard. He is working through those situations for your good and His glory. Each thing that your loving Heavenly Father allows to happen in your life is wise and good.

The Bible says, "How many are your works, O LORD! In wisdom you made them all..." (Psalm 104:24). God made everything and He knows everything. He loves you and wants you to trust Him completely. Will you trust Him today?

 How does God use His wisdom in your life?

_____

_____

_____

You can pray:

Dear God, You made everything and know everything. I will trust You today, knowing that everything that happens in my life is from You. In Jesus' name. Amen.

 hat Is the Fear of the Lord?

 ...let us be thankful, and so worship God acceptably with reverence and awe. **Hebrews 12:28**

Moses, the great leader of the Israelite people, was old and would soon die. One day he told the priests they should read the law to the people aloud every seven years. He said, "Assemble the people—men, women and children…so they can listen and learn to fear the LORD your God and follow carefully all the words of this law" (Deuteronomy 31:12). When the law was read, the people would learn more about God and His Word. The children would also hear the law and learn to fear and obey the Lord.

What does it mean to fear the Lord? It means that you become so aware of how holy and powerful God is that you are really afraid of disobeying Him. You do not want to displease God. When you fear God, you understand His greatness and you reverence Him—show Him respect and love. You think about Him with awe and wonder because of His great power. Fearing God also means that you worship Him, serve Him and trust Him.

Do you realize how really great and awesome God is? If you do, you will want to please and obey Him more than anything else.

How does God want you to fear Him?

_____

_____

_____

You can pray:

 Dear God, thank You for being my Heavenly Father and for loving me so much. Help me to please You in all things by obeying You. In Jesus' name. Amen.

H ow Do I Reverence God?

...let us be thankful, and so worship God acceptably with reverence and awe. **Hebrews 12:28**

How would you act if you were invited to visit a king? Would you run into his throne room laughing and talking? Would you ignore the king or call him by his first name? You would probably be quiet and respectful. What if you were invited to meet with the King of all kings, God Himself? How would you act? No doubt you would show Him great reverence.

To reverence God means to show loving respect for Him and His Word. You do not show reverence for God when you speak about Him in a careless way or use His name as a swear word. Because God is perfect and pure, it is a serious thing to Him when His children fail to reverence Him. You should not approach God lightly, as if He were not important. He is the most important one in all of the universe.

God is holy and He deserves your reverence. Be careful how you speak about God. Think about how holy God is before you use His name in a wrong way. Your reverence for God shows others that you have a special relationship with Him. Will you show honor and reverence for God today with your life?

Name three ways you can show reverence for God.

_____

_____

_____

You can pray:

Dear God, thank You that You are a great and holy God. Help me to reverence You today and every day. In Jesus' name. Amen.

26 What Does God Do for Me?

...let us be thankful, and so worship God acceptably with reverence and awe. **Hebrews 12:28**

All of us have needs— things we must have like food, clothing and shelter. Probably your parents take care of these things for you. But did you know that it is God who has provided so that your needs will be met?

God knows about your basic needs. He also knows you have the need to be loved, accepted and to feel safe and protected. Perhaps those who are supposed to take care of you have not been able to meet your needs. Your family might have to depend on others for help. At times, you may try to meet your own needs. But God wants you to look to Him first to provide for you.

He is your Heavenly Father who cares for you more than anyone else could.

There is no need too great or too hard for God to supply. He promises, "And my God will meet all your needs..." (Philippians 4:19). God has all of the riches in the world. He never lacks anything, so He is well able to supply any need.

God does not promise to supply everything you want, but your needs will never go unmet. Depend on God. Tell Him about your needs and trust Him to provide for you.

How does God take care of you?

_____

_____

_____

You can pray:

Dear God, thank You that You have the power to meet all my needs. Help me to trust You. In Jesus' name. Amen.

What Does God Do in the World?

...let us be thankful, and so worship God acceptably with reverence and awe. **Hebrews 12:28**

Have you ever wondered what God does all day? What in the world does God do? First, you know that God created the world and everything in it. The Bible says, "…You made the heavens, even the highest heavens, and all their starry host, the Earth and all that is on it, the seas and all that is in them. You give life to everything…" (Nehemiah 9:6). God is the owner of all.

Another thing that God does in the world is to rule over His creation. God has complete control over all things. He has control over the universe, the animals, the nations of the Earth and over people. He has control over nature—the sunshine, thunder, lightening, rain and snow. All nature obeys His will. God keeps everything in the world going according to His plan. He always has the good of His creation at heart.

Does it sometimes seem that God is not in control? Maybe it's because there are so many bad things happening in the world. God is taking care of all things. You don't need to worry because God is taking care of this big world and He's taking care of you!

Name two things that God does in the world.

_____

_____

_____

You can pray:

Dear God, thank You that You are in control of the world and everything in it. Help me to trust You and to not worry. In Jesus' name. Amen.

28

Do I Appreciate God?

...let us be thankful, and so worship God acceptably with reverence and awe. **Hebrews 12:28**

When someone does something nice for you, you normally say "thank you." You tell that person how much you appreciate what he or she did. Sometimes you may even buy the person a gift.

God has done so many wonderful things for you. He loves and cares for you. How do you tell Him that you appreciate all that He has done? One way is to give God honor. To give honor to God means to give Him a high place in your thinking. You also show honor when you tell others how great He is. The Bible says in Psalm 66:2, "Sing to the glory of his name; offer him glory and praise!" Instead of bragging when someone gives you a compliment, you honor God by saying, "Thank you. It was God who helped me." You are giving the honor to Him for what He does in your life.

God is the one who is worthy of our praise and honor. Will you honor Him today and every day? When God helps you, tell Him how much you appreciate His help. Let others know how great your Heavenly Father is. They will want to know Him, too.

How can you show God that you appreciate Him?

_____

_____

_____

You can pray:

Dear God, I love You and appreciate You. Thank You for all You have done for me. In Jesus' name. Amen.

oes God Know about Things in My Life? 29

 ...let us be thankful, and so worship God acceptably with reverence and awe. **Hebrews 12:28**

Have you ever tried to explain something to a friend, and he just stared at you? Maybe you think, *Doesn't anybody understand what I think or feel?*

God knows everything in the whole world, and God knows everything about you. The Bible says, "You [Lord] know when I sit and when I rise; you perceive [know] my thoughts...you are familiar with all my ways" (Psalm 139:2-3). God knows your thoughts and how you feel at any time of the day. He knows when you get up in the morning and when you go to bed. He sees your tears and hears your laughter. God knows when you're frustrated and when you're sad. He knows the tiniest movement that you make. He also knows every secret sin. Although God knows all about you, He still loves you!

Not one thing in your life goes unnoticed by God. Maybe no one else understands you and your situation, but God understands completely. He knows about your past, your present and your future. Because God knows the future, He can prepare you for it. Isn't it great to know that God knows all about you? Trust Him to do what is best in your life.

Name four things that God knows about you.

_____

_____

_____

You can pray:

 Dear God, thank You that You know all about me, and You love me. Help me to trust You to do what is best for me. In Jesus' name. Amen.

Does God Care about Me?

...let us be thankful, and so worship God acceptably with reverence and awe. **Hebrews 12:28**

Do you ever feel like no one cares about you? When hard things happen, you might feel like you're all alone. But there is someone who always cares. That someone is God.

If you know the Lord Jesus Christ as your Savior, you can trust God to take care of you. Perhaps when you get home from school you have to be alone while your parents are at work. Maybe you live where there is violence and you worry about being safe. It's natural to feel afraid sometimes—our world can be a very scary place! Do you think God knows about the dangers in your life? Yes, and He cares.

What should you do when you feel alone or scared? The Bible says, "Cast [put] all your anxiety [worries] on him [God] because he cares for you" (1 Peter 5:7). No matter what the problem is, God can take care of you.

Because you're His child, God has a plan for your life. He can work out any situation no matter how difficult it may be. When you're in a difficult situation, tell God about it. Think about how powerful He is—He can do anything! Thank Him that He loves and cares for you.

How do you know God cares for you?

_____

_____

_____

You can pray:

Dear God, thank You that You love and care for me. Help me to trust You in everything that happens. In Jesus' name. Amen.

H ow Can I Be Aware of God Each Day? 31

Let us be thankful, and so worship God acceptably with reverence and awe. **Hebrews 12:28**

David was a shepherd boy. He took care of his sheep far from home. He led his sheep to eat green grass and to drink fresh water. At times David played his harp. He loved God and made up songs about Him. David was always thinking about God.

Do you think about God during the day? Do you know that He is with you even though you can't see Him? You should think about Him many times every day. When you see the flowers or hear the birds sing, you can think about how wonderful God is. When you think about God while you're at school or at play, you will want to please Him.

If you are thinking about God while you play, you will not become angry or selfish. If you think about God while you do your school work, you will do a good job. If you think about God a lot, how can you do sinful things? How can you worry or be sad? The Bible says, "You [God] will keep in perfect peace him whose mind [thoughts] is steadfast [focused on God]" (Isaiah 26:3). God wants you to think of Him very often.

Name some specific times when you can think about God.

_____

_____

_____

You can pray:

Dear God, thank You that You are with me. Help me to think about You all the time and remember how great You are. In Jesus' name. Amen.

Will God Ever Change?

I the LORD do not change. **Malachi 3:6**

What if God suddenly decided He didn't want to be God anymore? How terrible if He stopped controlling our world. If God changed His mind about loving and forgiving us, we wouldn't be able to go on.

The good news is that this will never happen because God *never* changes! The Bible says, "...from everlasting to everlasting you are God" (Psalm 90:2). God doesn't grow older. He doesn't get new powers or lose the ones He has. He does not get stronger or weaker or wiser. He doesn't get better—He is already perfect!

God's Word will always be Truth. God will never change His mind about sin and forgiveness. He will never love you any more or any less than He does right now. He says, "I have loved you with an everlasting love" (Jeremiah 31:3).

Because God never changes, you can count on Him. He will always be there for you. He will always love and forgive you. He will always do what is best for you. He will always keep His promises to you. Best of all, you can look forward to being with Him forever in Heaven!

Finish this sentence: I am glad God never changes because...

_____

_____

_____

You can pray:

Dear God, thank You that You never change. Help me remember that You are always with me. Help me trust in Your promises. In Jesus' name. Amen.

The Trinity

The Lord is one God in three persons.
See if you can fill in the blanks below.

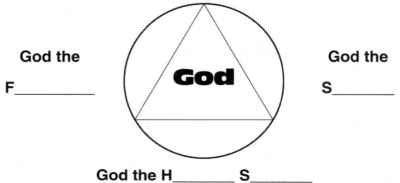

God the

F_____

God

God the

S_____

God the H_____ S_____

I show my reverence for God by… _____

_____

THINKING IT OVER!

1. What does it mean that God is eternal? _____

_____

2. What is sin? _____

_____

3. How can you be forgiven? _____

_____

4. What does "God is holy" mean? _____

_____

5. List two of God's rules for us: _____

_____

6. How can you know God will keep His promises? _____

_____

If you need help, you can look back in this month's devotionals. The number in ( ) tells you which devotional to check for each question. 1. (3)   2. (6)   3. (8)   4. (10)   5. (13)   6. (21)

hat Is Prophecy?

But when the time had fully come, God sent his Son....
Galatians 4:4

Can you imagine what it would be like to have God talk to you from Heaven? What would He sound like? What would He say?

Hundreds of years ago God talked to special men called "prophets." These men told others what God said. Sometimes they wrote it down for people to read. The prophets reminded people of God's great love for them. God also used the prophets to warn people to stop doing wrong or they would be punished.

God often told the prophets what was going to happen in the future. Since God knows everything, this was not hard for Him to do. The people knew it was a message from God. Only He could know these things.

Because God spoke through a prophet, the message was called a "prophecy." Many of these special messages can be found in the Bible. These messages were not just for the people then. They're for you and me today! God's most exciting messages were about His Son, Jesus. You'll learn what these were as you keep reading in the next few days.

Name something you are glad God already knows about.

_____

_____

_____

You can pray:

Dear God, thank You that You know all things, even before they happen. Help me to read Your Word every day. In Jesus' name. Amen.

Who Were God's Prophets?

 But when the time had fully come, God sent his Son.... **Galatians 4:4**

Who is the smartest person in the world? God, of course! He even knows what will happen in the future! The Bible says, "Lord, You know all things..." (John 21:17). Nothing surprises God! Have you ever wished you knew what was going to happen like God does?

Before the Lord Jesus came to Earth, God gave His chosen prophets special ability to know and write about the future. They told others what was going to happen. Many might have thought these men were very smart, but God's Holy Spirit told these prophets what to say. "...but men spoke from God as they were carried along by the Holy Spirit" (2 Peter 1:21). Whatever they said came true!

The first prophet to write a book in the Bible is Isaiah. His book is near the end of the Old Testament.

The prophets spoke to groups of people. They loved God and the people very much. Some people treated them badly when they shared God's messages. Others did not believe them. Many didn't like what they said. But these bold prophets did not quit sharing God's messages with others.

 How did the prophets have the boldness to share God's messages?

_____

_____

_____

You can pray:

 Dear God, help me to be bold like Your prophets when I tell others about You. Thank You for giving me the courage not to quit. In Jesus' name. Amen.

What Did God's Prophets Say about Jesus?

But when the time had fully come, God sent his Son....
Galatians 4:4

Do you like to read mysteries? A mystery is a secret that you figure out by using clues.

After God made the first man and woman, He promised to send a Savior to Earth. This special person would take the punishment for the wrong things they had done. The Savior also would be punished for your sins. No one knew who it would be. It was a mystery. But God gave clues to the prophets, His messengers. We find them written in the Old Testament of the Bible.

Here are just a few of many clues the prophets wrote. God's promised Savior would be born in the city of Bethlehem. He would be born in a stable—like a barn. He would be in the family of King David. He would be rejected by the people and killed! The prophets told how He would die and why. They even said He would come back to life! Who is the Promised Savior? You are right, the Lord Jesus Christ!

Some of these clues were written 700 years before Jesus ever came! There was no way the prophets could have known these things before they happened unless God had told them.

List three clues you learned about the Promised Savior.

_____

_____

_____

You can pray:

Dear God, I know Jesus is the one You promised to send. Thank You that He took the punishment for my sins. I believe in Jesus, Your Son! In Jesus' name. Amen.

**D**id God's Prophecies about Jesus Come True?

 But when the time had fully come, God sent his Son.... **Galatians 4:4**

"Could this be the Promised One from God?" many people wondered as they met the Lord Jesus! They had read the clues the prophets had written. They waited and watched. Then, at just the right time in history, Jesus came! "But when the time had fully come, God sent his Son."

One by one each clue the prophets had given about Jesus came true. Of all the cities in the world, He was born in Bethlehem. He was born in a stable. He was from the family of King David! Nazareth would become His hometown. All the prophecies about the Savior's birth had come true.

When He was grown, He did many amazing things that only God could do. But He was rejected by the people and treated very badly. He was nailed to a cross between two thieves. There He took the punishment for the sins of the whole world—including yours. All the prophecies about the Savior's death had come true. On the third day after Jesus died and was buried, He came back to life! Then, He returned to Heaven to be with His Father. The prophets had written all this and more. Jesus is the Promised One!

 Why don't some people believe Jesus is God's Promised Savior?

_____

_____

_____

You can pray:

 Dear God, thank You for sending the Lord Jesus to Earth at just the right time as You promised. You are a great God! In Jesus' name. Amen.

Is Jesus Really the Savior God Promised?

But when the time had fully come, God sent his Son....
Galatians 4:4

"**Follow me. I will help you get to Heaven.** Be good like me and someday you will be with God! I will show you the way." Many people have said this, but they were not telling the truth. Today, millions think men like Buddha or Mohammed will show them God's way. Others think they can find their own way to Heaven.

When Jesus lived on Earth, He said, "I am the way and the truth and the life. No one comes to the Father except through Me" (John 14:6). He was not only telling the truth, He was the truth! Only by believing (trusting) in Jesus, who died for your sins, can you be forgiven and come to God. Then, you can know you have life in Heaven with God forever.

Who did the Father send to Earth to be the Promised Savior? The Bible says, "...the Father has sent His Son to be the Savior of the world" (1 John 4:14). Savior means the one who saves us from our sins. Only Jesus was God's perfect Son. Only Jesus was punished for your sins. Only Jesus came back to life. Only Jesus is the Savior God promised.

Copy 1 John 4:14 below and say it to a friend.

_____

_____

_____

You can pray:

Dear God, I am glad I know the truth about Your Son, Jesus. Keep me from being tricked by others. In Jesus' name. Amen.

What Will Jesus Do in the Future?

38

But when the time had fully come, God sent his Son.... **Galatians 4:4**

When Jesus entered the city of Jerusalem, the people shouted, "...Blessed is...the King of Israel!" (John 12:13). The prophets had said the Promised Savior would someday rule the world. They thought that time had come, but Jesus hadn't come to Earth for that reason. He came to die for our sins. The people didn't understand this. They were sad and confused when Jesus did not become king right away. Instead, He was put to death on a cross.

However, Jesus came back to life again and lives in Heaven. God's Word says that someday Jesus will come back to rule the world as King. "When the Son of Man [Jesus] comes in his glory,...he will sit on the throne.... All the nations will be gathered before him..." (Matthew 25:31-32). Can you imagine what it will be like when Jesus is King? He is going to make a new earth. There will be no death, no tears, and no pain. What a wonderful place it will be!

All of those who have trusted the Lord Jesus as Savior will be with Him forever! Those who haven't will be separated from God in a terrible place of punishment. If you haven't yet trusted in Jesus as your Savior, you can pray the prayer below.

Write the date and place here when you trusted Jesus as your Savior.

_____

_____

_____

You can pray:

Dear God, I know I am a sinner. I believe in Jesus, who died to take the punishment for my sin and rose again. Please forgive my sins. In Jesus' name. Amen.

39

Why Does God Keep His Promises?

But when the time had fully come, God sent his Son....
Galatians 4:4

Have you ever made a promise you did not keep? "I promise I will be good from now on!" "I promise I will never speak to you again as long as I live!" "I promise I will never ask for another thing if you just get me what I want now!"

Has God ever made a promise He did not keep? No! God always keeps His promises because God is truth. You can believe what He says. Some things He told the prophets have not happened yet, but we know they will someday. The Bible says, "For the word of the Lord is right and true; he is faithful in all he does" (Psalm 33:4). We have already seen hundreds of prophecies come true, just as God promised!

The greatest promise God has made was to send Jesus to Earth. Why did God make that promise? God knew you needed a Savior. You have sinned and need to be forgiven. Why has God kept His promise? Because God is truth—He does not lie (Titus 1:2). Another reason He has kept His promise is because He loves you. You don't deserve His love or kindness, but because of Jesus, you can now be a child of God.

Write a poem to God, thanking Him for His love.

_____

_____

_____

You can pray:

Dear God, thank You for your love. I don't deserve Your love or kindness. You love me even when I sin. You are wonderful! I love You, too. In Jesus' name. Amen.

 **here Did Jesus Come From?**

 **46**

 In the beginning was the Word, and the Word was with God, and the Word was God. **John 1:1**

Before time began on Earth, the Bible says Jesus lived. He did not begin as a baby in Bethlehem. He was in Heaven before coming to Earth. He did not have a beginning, and He will live forever. How could this be? Because Jesus was, and is, God!

Jesus was not an angel who became God. He was not a man who later became like God. He has always been God. In fact, Jesus made the universe. "For by Him [Jesus] all things were created [made]: things in heaven and on earth…" (Colossians 1:16).

At just the right time in history, God sent His Son, Jesus, to be born as a baby so He could live on Earth like you and me. "The Word [Jesus] became flesh…" (John 1:14). While living on earth, Jesus proved He was God by His words and actions. He healed the sick, brought dead people back to life and calmed storms! He forgave sins and never once sinned!

During Jesus' life on Earth, God the Father spoke about Him from Heaven. God said, "This is my Son, whom I love; with him I am well pleased" (Matthew 3:17). God the Father wanted us to know for certain that Jesus truly is God the Son.

 Write down a verse from today's lesson that could help you explain who Jesus is.

_____

_____

_____

You can pray:

Dear God, I know Jesus is Your Son. Thank You for helping me know and believe the truth. In Jesus' name. Amen.

41 How Could Jesus Be Both God and Man?

In the beginning was the Word, and the Word was with God, and the Word was God. **John 1:1**

The King of the universe born as a baby? How could this be? That is exactly what happened. Jesus, God the Son, left His wonderful home in Heaven to come to Earth and be born as a baby. The Bible says, "The Word [Jesus] became flesh and made his dwelling [lived] among us…" (John 1:14). It was a miracle!

In Heaven, Jesus had all power and authority as God. When He became a human, Jesus willingly gave up His right to those things. He became like you and me. He got hungry, thirsty and tired. He felt pain and sadness. But because Jesus was still God the Son, He never sinned. He was completely God and man— perfect in every way.

Why did Jesus come to Earth as a human? He came to take your punishment for sin. "…[Jesus] humbled Himself and became obedient to death— even death on a cross!" (Philippians 2:8). He came to Earth to make a way for you to go to Heaven. Even when He was dying, there was never a moment that He was not God.

You don't have to understand how Jesus could be both God and man. You just need to believe that He was. God can do anything!

What are two things Jesus gave up when He came to Earth as a human?

_____

_____

_____

You can pray:

Dear God, even though I can't understand all about You and Your Son, Jesus, I believe what the Bible says. You are the mighty God! In Jesus' name. Amen.

# How Was Jesus Born?

**42**

In the beginning was the Word, and the Word was with God, and the Word was God. **John 1:1**

Mary was amazed at what she heard! An angel told her, "You will be with child and give birth to a son, and you are to give him the name Jesus. He will be great and will be called the Son of the Most High" (Luke 1:31-32). Mary didn't know how this could happen. She was a virgin. Without touching her in any physical way, God would place the baby within her. It was a miracle!

God gave Mary a husband named Joseph. He would help Mary take care of the baby Jesus. Joseph knew that God Himself was Jesus' real Father. An angel had visited Joseph, too, with the news. Perhaps he had read what the prophets had said about the coming Savior.

There was no room to stay in Bethlehem. Jesus was born in a stable. The Bible says, "...She [Mary] wrapped Him [Jesus] in cloths and placed Him in a manger [a feeding place for animals]" (Luke 2:7). This was all part of God's plan. Everything about His birth had come true, just as the prophets had said. This tiny baby lying in the manger was the Savior of the world!

Write down the words to your favorite Christmas song about baby Jesus.

_____

_____

_____

You can pray:

Dear God, thank You for sending Jesus to Earth in such a special way. It may not be Christmas now, but Happy Birthday, Jesus! In Jesus' name. Amen.

43 Was Jesus Like Me?

 In the beginning was the Word, and the Word was with God, and the Word was God. **John 1:1**

What was Jesus like as a boy? As the perfect Son of God, Jesus was different from you in many ways. But, there are some ways in which He was like you. He had a human body that got hungry and tired. He could be happy or sad.

Because He had a human body, He "grew in wisdom and stature, and in favor with God and men" (Luke 2:52). These are ways that you should be growing, too!

Jesus grew in "wisdom." When Jesus was twelve years old, He went to the temple (place of worship) where He talked with the religious leaders. They were impressed with His understanding and His answers. This story is in Luke 2:41-52.

Jesus grew in "stature." His body became bigger and His muscles grew stronger.

Jesus grew in "favor with God." Everything He did pleased His Father, God. Jesus knew His Father was watching and helping Him all the time!

Jesus grew in "favor with men." Others admired and respected Him.

Are you growing in these important ways? Are you making wise choices? Are you getting bigger and stronger? Are you pleasing God in all that you do? Do you treat others with respect and kindness?

 How can you grow to be more like Jesus?

_____

_____

_____

You can pray:

Dear God, help me to grow up to be like Your Son, Jesus. Thank You. In Jesus' name. Amen.

What Did Jesus Do on the Earth?

In the beginning was the Word, and the Word was with God, and the Word was God. **John 1:1**

"It's a miracle!" Jairus must have joyfully shouted. "My little girl was dead, but Jesus brought her back to life!" News spread quickly throughout the country (Matthew 9:18-26). Blind people could suddenly see (Luke 18:35-43). Crippled people could walk (Luke 5:17-26). Many sick people were being healed (Mark 6:53-56). And that's not all! Jesus walked on water (Mark 6:45-51). He made giant storms go away by simply speaking (Mark 4:35-41). Demons obeyed His commands (Matthew 17:14-18). Twice He fed thousands of people with just a little bit of food (John 6:3-13; Mark 8:1-10).

It seemed there was no limit to Jesus' mighty power! Whatever the problem, He could take care of it. These miracles showed God's power and love. Jesus was proving that He truly was the Son of God, just as the prophets had said!

The Bible says, "Jesus did many other things as well. If every one of them were written down, I suppose that even the whole world would not have room for the books that would be written" (John 21:25). What problem do you have in your life today? Whether it's big or small, Jesus can help! Tell Him about it and trust Him to do what's best for you.

Write down a big problem that Jesus can help you with.

_____

_____

_____

You can pray:

Dear God, Your power proves You can take care of my problems. Please help me to trust You with my problem today. In Jesus' name. Amen.

Why Is Jesus Called the Word?

In the beginning was the Word, and the Word was with God, and the Word was God. **John 1:1**

Words can be important! They tell others what you think, feel, or know to be true. Imagine a world without words!

The Bible says that Jesus "was the Word." This means that Jesus was God's message to you. Everything Jesus spoke told us how God thinks and feels. Everything Jesus did showed us what God would do.

Jesus was "the Word" as He taught how God wants you to think and behave. Not only did He say it, He showed you perfectly how to do it!

Jesus also taught about God's plan for you to have eternal life by believing on Him as your Savior. He is called "the Word of life." "That which was from the beginning, which we have heard, which we have seen with our eyes…and our hands have touched…the Word of life" (1 John 1:1).

When people listened and looked at Jesus, they were listening to and looking at God!

Since Jesus is God's message to you, it is very important that you know Him! What Jesus said and did is found in the books of Matthew, Mark, Luke and John in the Bible. Other books may help you, too, like this devotional book.

What have you learned about Jesus that you didn't know before?

_____

_____

_____

You can pray:

Dear God, help me get to know You better every day. In Jesus' name. Amen.

Was Jesus Ever Tempted to Sin

 In the beginning was the Word, and the Word was with God, and the Word was God. **John 1:1**

Have you ever wanted to be perfect? Maybe you have even tried. If someone told you he or she was perfect, I am sure you would watch very carefully for proof!

When Jesus lived on Earth, He proved He was perfect! Satan tempted Him many times to do wrong, but He never did! One day Satan visited Jesus in a wilderness in Judea. "If you are the Son of God," he taunted, "tell these stones to become bread" (Matthew 4:3). He was tempting Jesus not to follow God's plan.

Two other times Satan tempted Jesus to become proud and show His power. Satan even tried to get Jesus to worship him! Jesus knew God's plan for His coming to Earth, and this was not it! He was determined to do only what His Father wanted.

Did Jesus ever give in? No! He could not sin, for He was God's perfect Son. He was exactly who He claimed to be, and He proved it! Jesus spoke the truth to Satan from God's Word. Satan eventually left Him.

Jesus proved many times His power over Satan. That is why the Lord Jesus can help you when you are tempted to do wrong.

 What can you do when you are tempted to sin?

_____

_____

_____

You can pray:

 Dear God, please help me when I am tempted to disobey You. I will depend on Your power to say "no." In Jesus' name. Amen.

47 What Happened in the Room Upstairs?

For God so loved the world that he gave his one and only Son, that whoever believes in him shall not perish but have eternal life. **John 3:16**

It was the night before Jesus was to be killed. His thirty-three years on Earth were almost over. The special Jewish holiday called the Passover had come. The prophets had said this would be the time of His death. Jesus met with his twelve close followers in an upstairs room for their last meal together (Luke 22:7-23).

The bread and wine Jesus passed to His disciples that night had special meaning. The next day He would die on a cross. The bread and wine were to be reminders of His wounded body and His blood that would flow on the cross as payment for our sins. Judas was there eating with Him. Before the meal was over, Judas left the room to go and betray Jesus by leading His enemies to Him. (John 13:21-30)

Jesus made some wonderful promises to His followers. Then, they sang one last song together and left. It was a night they would never forget.

Jesus told His followers to continue to remember His death in the same way He had demonstrated in the upstairs room. Today we call this Communion or the Lord's Supper. We are to remember His death in this way until He comes again.

How was the night in the upstairs room important for us today?

_____

_____

_____

You can pray:

Dear God, thank You for giving this special way to remember what Jesus did for me. In Jesus' name. Amen.

hy Was Jesus on Trial?

For God so loved the world that he gave his one and only Son, that whoever believes in him shall not perish but have eternal life. **John 3:16**

The night in the upstairs room had been special to Jesus and His disciples. But the religious leaders who hated Jesus wanted to have Him killed! Why? Because Jesus had said He was the Son of God. He claimed to be the Messiah—the one God promised to send into the world to save everyone from sin. The leaders refused to believe Him. They arrested Jesus and put Him on trial.

Since Jesus had done nothing wrong, the religious leaders had to get men to tell lies about Him. For hours, Jesus listened to their lies and He was painfully beaten. The religious leaders wanted Jesus put to death, so they took Him to Pilate, the governor. "He has claimed to be the Son of God!" the leaders declared. "For this He must die!" Jesus did not say a word. (John 19:7-9)

Pilate asked Jesus, "Don't you realize I have power either to free you or to crucify you?" Jesus answered, "You would have no power over me if it were not given to you from above" (John 19:11). Jesus knew that being on trial was part of God's plan. The time had come for Him to suffer and die for the sins of the world.

 If you had been at Jesus' trial, what would you have told about Jesus?

_____

_____

_____

You can pray:

Dear God, I believe Jesus is Your Son, just as He said. Thank You that He was willing to suffer and die for my sin. In Jesus' name. Amen.

Where Were Jesus' Friends?

 For God so loved the world that he gave his one and only Son, that whoever believes in him shall not perish but have eternal life. **John 3:16**

Before Jesus was arrested and put on trial, He had talked with one of His disciples named Peter. Jesus told Peter, "'…this very night, before the rooster crows, you will disown [deny] me three times.' But Peter declared. 'Even if I have to die with you, I will never disown you!' And all the other disciples said the same" (Matthew 26:34-35). But that night, when Jesus was arrested, his disciples ran away. They were afraid.

Peter followed at a distance. It was a horrible sight! Jesus was accused of things He didn't do. He was whipped, beaten, slapped, punched, mocked and spit upon. One could hardly recognize Him because of the bruises and blood.

Peter sat outside, warming himself by the fire. A servant girl pointed to him and said, "You also were with Jesus…" (Matthew 26:69).

"I don't know what you're talking about," Peter replied (Matthew 26:70). Two other servants said they recognized Peter as one of Jesus' followers, but two more times Peter denied that he knew Jesus. Then the rooster crowed. As Jesus was led out of the trial, He looked at Peter, and Peter remembered Jesus' words. How could he have denied Jesus? Peter went away, crying bitterly.

 Write about a time when you spoke up for Jesus, even though it was hard.

_____

_____

_____

You can pray:

 Dear God, I am sorry for the times I have pretended not to know You. Help me to be brave to speak up for You. In Jesus' name. Amen.

Why Did Jesus Have to Die?

 For God so loved the world that he gave his one and only Son, that whoever believes in him shall not perish but have eternal life. **John 3:16**

Jesus' arms were stretched out as soldiers nailed him to a wooden cross. The pain was horrible. The Lord Jesus was being crucified.

The mocking crowd said, "Come down from the cross, if you are the Son of God!" (Matthew 27:42). Because Jesus was the Son of God, He would not come down. God the Father placed on His perfect Son the sin of the whole world. "God made him [Jesus] who had no sin to be sin for us…" (2 Corinthians 5:21). Jesus willingly bled and died on the cross to take the punishment that God required for sin.

Hours later, darkness came over the whole countryside. Jesus cried out, "My God, My God, why have you forsaken Me?" (Matthew 27:45). The perfect, holy God could not look at His Son, who had taken upon Himself the sin of the world.

Later Jesus said, "Father, into Your hands I commit My spirit!" (Luke 23:46), and Jesus died. Some of the soldiers who had seen all that had happened said, "Surely he was the Son of God!" (Matthew 27:54). When Jesus took the punishment for sin on the cross, He did all that was necessary to be called the Savior.

 Finish this sentence: Jesus had to die because…

_____

_____

_____

You can pray:

 Dear God, thank You for being willing to send Your Son to die in my place. In Jesus' name. Amen.

Who Moved the Stone?

For God so loved the world that he gave his one and only Son, that whoever believes in him shall not perish but have eternal life. **John 3:16**

A friend named Joseph asked for permission to take Jesus' dead body down from the cross and bury Him. After His body was wrapped in special cloths, they placed Him in a tomb, or cave. A huge stone, requiring several men to move it, was rolled in front of the entrance. The religious leaders asked Pilate to assign armed soldiers to guard the tomb day and night. (Matthew 27:57-65)

Suddenly, on the third day, there was an earthquake! An angel came down from Heaven and rolled the stone from the door! The guards shook with fear and fell down as if they were dead. A few women, who were Jesus' friends came to visit the tomb. They brought spices to put on Jesus' body, but when they arrived, the women were surprised to see a shining angel sitting on top of the stone! The tomb was empty! Jesus was gone! (Matthew 28:1-4)

The angel said, "Do not be afraid, for I know that you are looking for Jesus, who was crucified. He is not here; he has risen, just as he said…go quickly and tell His disciples he has risen from the dead…" (Matthew 28:5-7). The women ran to tell the disciples.

What would you have said to Jesus the day He came back to life?

_____

_____

_____

You can pray:

Dear God, because Your Son came back to life, I can live forever with You in Heaven! You are an awesome God! In Jesus' name. Amen.

Can I Know for Sure That I Am Forgiven?

For God so loved the world that he gave his one and only Son, that whoever believes in him shall not perish but have eternal life. John 3:16

Have you ever wondered if you are really forgiven? One of the last things Jesus said as He hung on the cross was, "It is finished!" He meant that He had done all that is necessary to pay for your sin. God loved you when you didn't deserve it. Jesus died for you so you could be forgiven. If you have trusted Jesus as your Savior, God kept His promise. He has forgiven you, and you have eternal life. One Bible writer says, "I write these things to you who believe in the name of the Son of God so that you may **know** that you have eternal life" (1 John 5:13). Also, the Bible says that when God forgives you, He won't remember your sins anymore (Hebrews 8:12).

Maybe you're thinking, *But I don't feel like I'm forgiven!* Your forgiveness does not depend on how you feel. It is based on your faith in Jesus and what He has done for you. Put your name in His promise: "For God so loved [your name] that he gave his one and only Son, that if [your name] believes in him [your name] shall not perish but have eternal life" (John 3:16).

 How do you know you are forgiven?

_____

_____

_____

You can pray:

Dear God, thank You for keeping Your promise to me. Thank You for forgiving me and for the gift of eternal life. In Jesus' name. Amen.

What Can I Give to God?

For God so loved the world that he gave his one and only Son, that whoever believes in him shall not perish but have eternal life. **John 3:16**

If you've received the Lord Jesus Christ as your Savior, you're probably just beginning to realize the wonderful gift He is! Jesus is your friend and helper. He is God's free gift to you!

When someone gives you a wonderful gift, you usually want to give that person something in return. Perhaps you are so grateful for God's gift of the Lord Jesus that you would like to give Him something special. But what do you give to God, who owns everything? The gift He wants most is you! One of the Bible writers said, "I urge [plead with] you, brothers, in view of God's mercy, to offer your bodies as living sacrifices, holy and pleasing to God" (Romans 12:1).

A sacrifice is an offering or gift. You can tell God you want to give yourself to Him. Give Him your eyes and ears, your feet and your hands. Give Him your mind and your heart. Give Him every part of you to do what pleases Him. Why should you present your body to God? Because you love Him. He wants you to be holy, set apart, for Him to use in whatever way He chooses. Will you give yourself to God now?

Write a thank you note to God for His gift to you.

_____

_____

_____

You can pray:

Dear God, I give myself to You. I will go where You want me to go, do what You want me to do and be what You want me to be. In Jesus' name. Amen.

Did Jesus Really Come Back to Life?

 ...Christ died for our sins according to the Scriptures, that He was buried, that He was raised on the third day according to the Scriptures.... **1 Corinthians 15:3-4**

"**Jesus, alive from the dead? I'll prove it's not true!**" Many people have said this from the first day Jesus came back to life. Some are still saying it today! Maybe you've also wondered if Jesus truly came alive again. He did! And there is much evidence to prove it is true.

Some have tried to prove Jesus didn't really die. They say He just fainted and that His disciples pretended that He died and came alive again. But Jesus' enemies made sure He was dead before His body was taken down from the cross. They also made sure no one could steal His body and pretend He had risen.

After Jesus came back to life, over five hundred people saw Him on at least fifteen different occasions! They touched Him, talked to Him and ate with Him. Many of these witnesses were tortured and killed by Jesus' enemies. If it were not true, they certainly would have said so to save their own lives.

For hundreds of years, millions of people all over the world have testified that Jesus is alive! Even though we can no longer see Him with our eyes, we can see Jesus changing lives and answering our prayers.

 How do you know that Jesus is alive?

_____

_____

_____

You can pray:

 Dear God, thank You that Jesus is alive, and that He is working in my life today. In Jesus' name. Amen.

What Were Jesus' Last Words?

...Christ died for our sins according to the Scriptures, that He was buried, that He was raised on the third day according to the Scriptures.... **1 Corinthians 15:3-4**

If you were not going to see your family and friends for a very long time, what would you say to them? I am sure you would choose your words very carefully. It would be important for them to remember your last instructions.

After Jesus came back to life, He stayed on earth for forty more days (Acts 1:3). Then, it was time for Him to return to Heaven. His family and friends would not see Him for a very long time. What were Jesus' last words to those He loved? "Go into all the world and preach the good news to all creation" (Mark 16:15).

Jesus' instructions are for you and me as well. Tell others everywhere the good news about the Lord Jesus Christ. He died, taking the punishment for your sin. He came back to life three days later. Now anyone can believe in Him and receive His gift of everlasting life.

Do you know someone who needs to hear about Jesus? Plan a time to tell him or her. Do you know others who are sharing the good news about Jesus? Perhaps you could pray or give money to help them.

Who will you share the good news about Jesus with this week?

_____

_____

_____

You can pray:

Dear God, help me to tell others about You. Also, use me to help others share Your good news. In Jesus' name. Amen.

 ow Did Jesus Return to Heaven?

 ...Christ died for our sins according to the Scriptures, that He was buried, that He was raised on the third day according to the Scriptures.... **1 Corinthians 15:3-4**

One day, Jesus had taken His disciples up on a mountain. He had finished giving His last instructions to them. Now it was time for Him to return to Heaven. Suddenly, as the disciples watched in silent amazement, Jesus began rising into the air. As He rose higher and higher, the disciples had to strain their eyes to see Him. Finally, a cloud hid Him from their sight. It was amazing! Jesus' mighty power had taken Him back to His home in Heaven. (Acts 1:9-10)

As the disciples continued to stare into the sky, two angels appeared and spoke to them. "This same Jesus, who has been taken from you into heaven, will come back in the same way you have seen him go into Heaven" (Acts 1:11). One day Jesus will return from Heaven in the clouds!

What did the disciples do next? First, they worshiped the Lord Jesus. Then, they returned to the city with great joy (Luke 24:52). Can you imagine how the disciples felt telling others what they had just seen? What an exciting day it had been. And how exciting to know that, one day, Jesus will return!

What would you have done if you had seen Jesus go up into Heaven?

_____

_____

_____

You can pray:

 Dear God, I'm glad You are alive in Heaven! Help me to tell the good news about You to others. In Jesus' name. Amen.

57 What Is Jesus Doing in Heaven?

...Christ died for our sins according to the Scriptures, that He was buried, that He was raised on the third day according to the Scriptures.... **1 Corinthians 15:3-4**

About 2,000 years have passed since the Lord Jesus Christ left the Earth to return to Heaven. What has He been doing all this time? One thing He's been doing is to prepare a beautiful home for His children! Jesus promised, "In my Father's house [Heaven] are many rooms...I am going there to prepare a place for you" (John 14:2).

Will this home look like a fine house in Asia, Africa or America? Will it look like a grand castle in Europe or a beautiful island home? We can't begin to imagine! Nothing on Earth will come close to its beauty! A perfect God who loves you very much is making this perfect place!

Not only is the Lord Jesus preparing a place for you, He is preparing you for that place! He wants you to be ready to enjoy all that He is making for you. For this reason, He is also praying for you. "Christ Jesus...is at the right hand of God and is also interceding [praying] for us" (Romans 8:34). Isn't it wonderful to know that Jesus is thinking about you right now? He loves you, He prays for you and He looks forward to being with you forever!

What do you think your place in Heaven might look like?

_____

_____

_____

You can pray:

Dear God, thank You for preparing a special place just for me. Thank You for praying for me so I will be ready for that special place. In Jesus' name. Amen.

Is Jesus Really Praying for Me?

...Christ died for our sins according to the Scriptures, that He was buried, that He was raised on the third day according to the Scriptures.... **1 Corinthians 15:3-4**

Yes! Jesus is praying for you. One thing He is praying is that you will stand strong against the temptation to sin. Jesus remembers what it was like when Satan tempted Him on Earth. He knows that you still have that "want to" to sin. He prays that you will say "no" to temptation.

The Bible says that Satan stands before God's throne, day and night, accusing us of our sins (Revelation 12:10). Every time we give in to sin, Satan points out our guilt to God. That's when the Lord Jesus speaks to God the Father for us. The Bible says, "...we have one who speaks to the Father in our defense—Jesus Christ, the Righteous one" (1 John 2:1). Jesus, the perfect One, is like your lawyer. He tells the judge, God the Father, that you are not guilty because He already paid for your sin by dying on the cross. No accusation from Satan can stand up to Jesus' defense!

When God declares you "not guilty" and He forgives you, it's not because you deserve it. God is being merciful to you because of His Son, Jesus, who has prayed for you. Aren't you glad that the Lord Jesus prays for you every day?

Why do you need Jesus to pray for you?

_____

_____

_____

You can pray:

Dear God, thank You for Jesus, who prays for me. Thank You for Your forgiveness. In Jesus' name. Amen.

When Will Jesus Return to Earth?

...Christ died for our sins according to the Scriptures, that He was buried, that He was raised on the third day according to the Scriptures.... **1 Corinthians 15:3-4**

Suddenly, when we least expect it, Jesus will come back to Earth! The prophets foretold that Jesus would come the first time, and He did. The prophets have also told us to look for His coming again. The Bible says, "For the Lord Himself will come down from heaven, with a loud command, with the voice of the archangel and with the trumpet call of God…" (1 Thessalonians 4:16). Jesus Himself also promised His return to Earth someday. "And if I go and prepare a place for you, I will come back and take you to be…where I am" (John 14:3). He is coming to take His children home to Heaven.

When will it happen? He didn't say. It could happen any day at any time. The Bible does tell us certain events to look for that would be clues to Jesus' return. His coming could take place in your lifetime! If you have not trusted the Lord Jesus as your Savior, this could be frightening news! You will be left to endure much suffering. But you can trust in Him today! If you have already trusted the Lord Jesus Christ as your Savior, you should be excited about seeing Him face to face!

If you knew Jesus was coming today, how would you spend your time?

_____

_____

_____

You can pray:

Dear God, thank You that Jesus is coming back again. Help me to be ready for His return. In Jesus' name. Amen.

How Can I Be Ready for Jesus' Return?

...Christ died for our sins according to the Scriptures, that He was buried, that He was raised on the third day according to the Scriptures.... **1 Corinthians 15:3-4**

If you have ever taken a trip, you know it is important to prepare. Right now you need to prepare for your trip to Heaven. If you've never trusted Jesus Christ as your Savior, now is the time to do that. The Bible says, "...now is the time of God's favor, now is the day of salvation" (2 Corinthians 6:2). Tell God you are sorry for your sin. Thank the Lord Jesus for taking your punishment for sin on the cross. Ask Him to make you His child. Don't wait; you may not get another chance.

If you have already trusted the Lord Jesus as your Savior, now is the time to get to know God better. Now is the time to obey His Word. The Bible says, "And now, dear children, continue in him [stay close to Jesus], so that when he appears we may be confident and unashamed before him at his coming" (1 John 2:28). If you are living close to Jesus Christ, you will not be ashamed to see Him when He appears. Look back over the devotionals in this book to remind yourself of other things you can do to prepare for your trip to Heaven.

What can you do today to get ready for your trip to Heaven?

_____

_____

_____

You can pray:

Dear God, thank You that I can be with you in Heaven someday. Help me to prepare now for the day I will see You. In Jesus' name. Amen.